MW01703538

Easy CABLE Throws™

Table of Contents

Welcome

Come and join in on all the fun and satisfaction that knitters gain when they succeed in knitting their first cable. Many knitters avoid patterns that have cables because they think cables look difficult. Cables may look complex, but, in reality, they are very easy to knit.

Learning to stitch cables by knitting a throw is the best way to learn and practice cables. A throw has no shaping, and you really don't have to worry about the gauge. You can focus on knitting cables. A throw also gives you lots of practice in stitching cables, unlike dishcloths and sweaters which usually have only one or two cables that go a short distance.

Before you start, you will need to purchase a cable needle. Any kind will work. For a cable with more stitches, use a larger cable needle, for a cable with fewer stitches, use a smaller cable needle. I recommend you try several kinds to find out which one works best for you.

If counting rows is not something you enjoy doing, you will also want to purchase a row counter. This tool is especially helpful if you are knitting more than one kind of cable in the same throw. Once you have these tools, you are ready to start your first project.

Start with the first throw in the book and work your way to the end. The last throw in the book, the Rose Aran Throw, has multiple cables and would be difficult for a beginner. By the time you have stitched your way through all the throws in the book, you will be an old hand at knitting

cables and will be able to knit this throw without any problems. In addition, you will have a stack of gorgeous throws to use in your home or to share with others. Never again will you pass on a knitting design because it has a cable in it.

So, welcome to the world of cables. Soon you will telling your fellow knitters that cables aren't difficult. Anyone can do them. They just take a little practice. Happy knitting!

Learn to Knit Cables

A single twisting cable or a combination of cables adds texture and interest to any knit piece. Cables are made by changing the order or position of the stitches on the needle with the use of a cable needle. It is not really difficult to do—just slip some of the stitches onto the cable needle and hold them out of the way, work additional stitches, then work the stitches from the cable needle and continue on your way! The frequency of the twist, the holding position and the way the twists are combined are what create the beautiful and seemingly complicated patterns.

This book contains a variety of cable patterns from a simple single twist in the *Super-Sized Cables*, to numerous cables twisted over different numbers of stitches on different rows in the *Rose Aran Throw*.

Cables can continue to be twisted in the same direction with each twist as in the *For Men Only Throw*. They can also form a "snake-like" pattern by alternately twisting one way and then the other as in the *Cables & Lace Throw* where the cable is combined with an all-over lace pattern. There seem to be endless ways to use and combine cables.

Cables can be worked side-by-side as in the *Rose Aran Throw* or set off with the use of Moss stitch or garter stitches between the cables as in the *Comfy Ribbed Cables Throw* and *Hugs & Kisses for Baby*.

While the number of twists and cables may increase, the means of making the cable remains the same. Included are step-by-step instructions for making the twists and charts that help in visualizing the process. If this is your first try at cables you might want to start with the *For Men Only Throw*. If you are more experienced, pick your favorite project and let's start twisting!

SUPPLIES FOR MAKING CABLES

To the right is a photo of some helpful accessories for making cables.

Cable Needles

Cable needles come in a variety of shapes and sizes to accommodate various types of yarn, but all are meant for the same task—that of holding stitches either in front or in back of the work and out of the way while other stitches are worked. They are made with a point at both ends so stitches can be slipped on at one end and worked off at the other. Most have an area in the middle to hold the stitches so they won't slip off.

Stitch Markers

Stitch markers also come in different sizes to fit a variety of needle sizes. Markers are used when a single cable is worked by itself or when multiple cables are separated by other stitches. The markers are placed on the needle on each side of the cable to "set it off." As the pattern is only worked on the stitches between the markers, this prevents continued counting of the stitches between the cables. The markers are slipped from one needle to the other when working across the row.

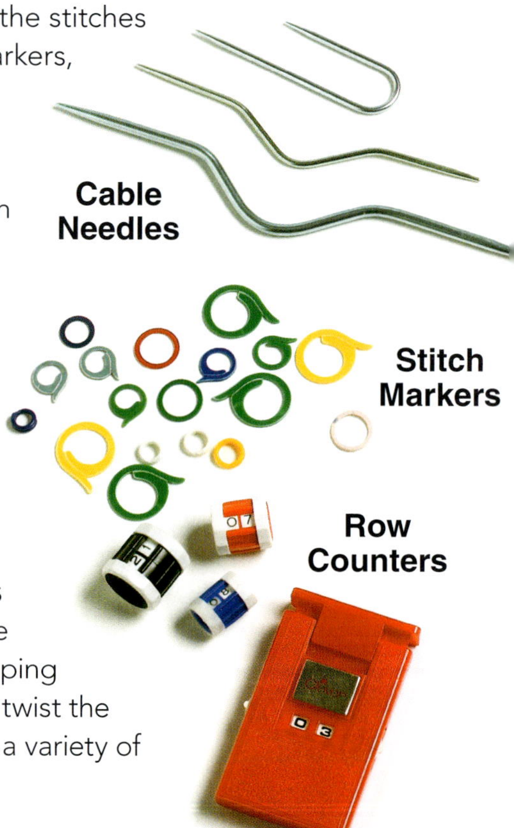

Row Counters

Row counters are invaluable in keeping track of when to twist the cable. There are a variety of types available. Some slip onto the needle and the number is turned each time a row is completed. Others are separate and clicked each time a row is finished. Sometimes a self-adhesive piece of paper and pencil with tally marks will do the trick. Regardless of the method, it is very important to keep track of the rows especially when first starting so that the cables are twisted consistently.

TWISTING THE CABLE

The most common cable used in this book is the Cable 4 Back (C4B). This is the cable pattern that is worked over 4 stitches.

To work Cable 4 Back (C4B):
Slip next 2 sts onto cable needle and hold in back of work.

Knit next 2 sts from left-hand needle.

Knit 2 sts from cable needle completing the C4B.

Continuing to work this pattern and twisting the cable in the same manner each time creates a cable that twists to the right.

To work Cable 4 Front (C4F):
Slip next 2 sts onto cable needle and hold in front of the work instead of in back.

Complete the cable in the same manner as the Cable 4 Back.

When the cables are always twisted in this manner the cable twists to the left.

If the direction of the twist is alternated a "snake-like" twist occurs.

This is all there is to twisting the cable: slip some stitches onto the needle, holding them either in front or in back, work additional stitches, then work the stitches from the cable needle.

WORKING FROM CHARTS

Reading Symbols

In addition to providing written instructions for the cable pattern stitches, charts have also been used for some patterns. On these charts, symbols are used to represent the various cable patterns and help give a visual image of the design. As there is no standard for these symbols, it is wise to check the stitch key given to become familiar with the symbols used.

The chart is read from bottom to top. On the chart each square represents a stitch. Right side or odd-numbered rows are usually read across the chart from right to left, and wrong side or even-numbered rows are usually read from left to right. When there is no symbol in the box, the stitch is knitted on the right side and purled on the wrong side. If the box has a black circle in it, the stitch is purled on the right side and knitted on the wrong side.

When first starting, it may be easiest to follow the written instructions for the pattern stitch while referring to the chart. However, after repeating the pattern several times, it may be easier to refer only to the chart.

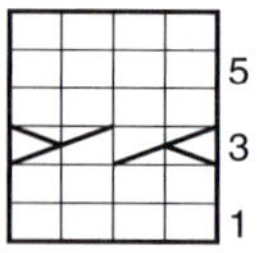

CABLE BACK PATTERN CHART

As Row 1 is a right side row and the chart squares are empty, Row 1 would be a knit row. Row 2 is a wrong side row and the squares are also empty, so Row 2 would be a purl row. Row 3 contains the symbol for a C4B or Cable 4 Back. In the instructions under the pattern stitch, it specifies how to make each cable or twist pattern. In this case, sl the next 2 sts onto the cable needle and hold them in back of the work, K2 sts, then K2 sts from the cable needle to make the C4B. Returning to the chart, Rows 4, 5 and 6 are left empty, so even-numbered rows are purled and odd-numbered rows are knit. Once you have finished the last row at the top of the chart begin again with Row 1.

Using Repeats

For some of these patterns, the chart is used for a single cable pattern that is worked in a specific area of the piece with other stitches to set it off. Other patterns are worked by repeating the cable pattern across the entire working area. In this case, a portion of the chart continues to be repeated. Below is the chart for the *Honeycomb Cable* featured in the *Rose Aran Throw*.

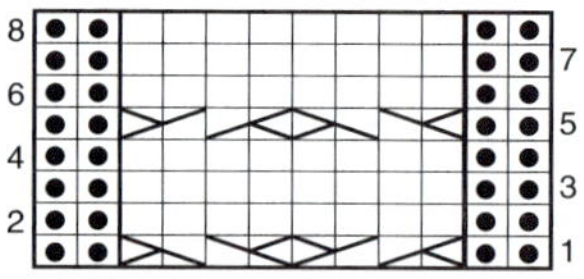

Rep Rows 1–8 for pat

HONEYCOMB CABLE

Notice that on Row 1 the C4B is worked followed by a C4F. The C4B-C4F combination is repeated across the row. Sometimes red lines are used to set off the repeat and act as an asterisk indicating that what is within those lines is repeated.

STITCH GAUGE

While the stitch gauge for these patterns is given in stockinette or garter stitch, this is only a guideline. A cable causes the piece to pull in. The more cables and twists, the more the piece shrinks in width. In the photo below, the same number of stitches have been worked. On the left, these stitches were worked in stockinette stitch; on the right, the same number of stitches were worked in a cable pattern. Note that the piece on the right, is narrower.

The need for additional stitches to accommodate the shrinkage has been taken into account when designing the throws. ■

Standard Abbreviations

[ ] work instructions within brackets as many times as directed
( ) work instructions within parentheses in the place directed
****** repeat instructions following the asterisks as directed
***** repeat instructions following the single asterisk as directed
" inch(es)
approx approximately
beg begin/beginning
CC contrasting color
ch chain stitch
cm centimeter(s)
cn cable needle
dec decrease/decreases/decreasing
dpn(s) double-pointed needle(s)
g gram
inc increase/increases/increasing
k knit
k2tog knit 2 stitches together
LH left hand
lp(s) loop(s)
m meter(s)
M1 make one stitch
MC main color
mm millimeter(s)
oz ounce(s)
p purl
pat(s) pattern(s)
p2tog purl 2 stitches together
psso pass slipped stitch over
p2sso pass 2 slipped stitches over
rem remain/remaining
rep repeat(s)
rev St st reverse stockinette stitch
RH right hand
rnd(s) rounds
RS right side
skp slip, knit, pass stitch over—one stitch decreased
sk2p slip 1, knit 2 together, pass slip stitch over the knit 2 together—2 stitches have been decreased
sl slip
sl 1k slip 1 knitwise
sl 1p slip 1 purlwise
sl st slip stitch(es)
ssk slip, slip, knit these 2 stitches together—a decrease
st(s) stitch(es)
St st stockinette stitch/stocking stitch
tbl through back loop(s)
tog together
WS wrong side
wyib with yarn in back
wyif with yarn in front
yd(s) yard(s)
yfwd yarn forward
yo yarn over

For Men Only Throw

dbl yarn

SIZE

Approx 44 inches x 60 inches

MATERIALS

- Caron Simply Soft 100 percent acrylic worsted weight yarn (330 yds/170g per skein): 8 skeins country blue #9710
- Size 13 (9mm) 32-inch circular knitting needle
- Cable needle

GAUGE

10 sts and 14 rows = 4 inches/10 cm in St st with 2 strands of yarn held tog
Gauge is not crucial in this project.

SPECIAL ABBREVIATIONS

M1 (Make 1): Insert LH needle from front to back into strand between st just worked and next st, k1-tbl.

C4B (Cable 4 Back): Sl next 2 sts onto cn and hold in back of work, k2, k2 from cn.

C4F (Cable 4 Front): Sl next 2 sts onto cn and hold in front of work, k2, k2 from cn.

PATTERN STITCHES

A. Left Cable (worked over 4 sts)

Rows 1, 5 and 7 (RS): Knit.

Rows 2, 4 and 6: Purl.

Row 3: C4F.

Row 8: Purl.

Rep Rows 1–8 for pat.

B. Right Cable (worked over 4 sts)

Rows 1, 5 and 7 (RS): Knit.

Rows 2, 4 and 6: Purl.

Row 3: C4B.

Row 8: Purl.

Rep Rows 1–8 for pat.

C. Center Cable (worked over 10 sts)

Rows 1, 5 and 7 (RS): Knit.

Rows 2, 4 and 6: Purl.

Row 3: C4B, k2, C4F.

Row 8: Purl.

Rep Rows 1–8 for pat.

PATTERN NOTES

Circular needle is used to accommodate stitches. Do not join; work back and forth in rows.

Charts are provided (page 10) for the pat sts for those preferring to work from charts.

Cables to the left of the center twist to the right while the cables to the right of the center twist to the left to mirror each other.

The 3-st garter st border requires occasional short rows in order to keep border flat. These short rows are worked every 8 rows. An easy way to remember this is that it happens every time the 8-row cable is twisted.

INSTRUCTIONS

Holding 2 strands of yarn together throughout, long-tail cast on 104 sts.

Lower Border

Knit 4 rows.

Inc Row (WS): K14, [M1, k12] 3 times, M1, k5, [M1, k12] 4 times, k1. (112 sts)

Body

Row 1 (RS): K3, [p9, work Row 1 of Right Cable over next 4 sts] 3 times, p9, work Row 1 of Center Cable over next 10 sts, p9, [work Row 1 of Left Cable over next 4 sts, p9] 3 times, k3.

Row 2: K3, [k9, work Row 2 of Left Cable] 3 times, k9, work Row 2 of Center Cable, k9, [work Row 2 of Right Cable, k9] 3 times, k3.

Row 3 (short row and cable-turning row): K3, sl 1 wyib, bring yarn forward between needles, turn; leaving rem sts unworked, sl 1 wyib, k3, turn, k3, [p9, work Row 3 of Right Cable over next 4 sts] 3 times, p9, work Row 3 of Center Cable over next 10 sts, p9, [work Row 3 of Left Cable over next 4 sts, p9] 3 times, k3, turn; k3, sl 1 wyib, bring yarn forward between needles, turn; sl 1 wyib, k3.

Row 4: K3, [k9, work Row 4 of Left Cable] 3 times, k9, work Row 4 of Center Cable, k9, [work Row 4 of Right Cable, k9] 3 times, k3.

Row 5: K3, [p9, work Row 5 of Right Cable over next 4 sts] 3 times, p9, work Row 5 of Center Cable over next 10 sts, p9, [work Row 5 of Left Cable over next 4 sts, p9] 3 times, k3.

Row 6: K3, [k9, work Row 6 of Left Cable] 3 times, k9, work Row 6 of Center Cable, k9, [work Row 6 of Right Cable, k9] 3 times, k3.

Row 7: K3, [p9, work Row 7 of Right Cable over next 4 sts] 3 times, p9, work Row 7 of Center Cable over next 10 sts, p9, [work Row 7 of Left Cable over next 4 sts, p9] 3 times, k3.

Row 8: K3, [k9, work Row 8 of Left Cable] 3 times, k9, work Row 8 of Center Cable, k9, [work Row 8 of Right Cable, k9] 3 times, k3.

Rep Rows 1–8 until piece measures approx 58½ inches from beg, ending with Row 3 of pattern.

Upper Border

Dec Row (WS): K13, [k2tog, k11] 3 times, k2tog, k4, k2tog, [k11, k2tog] 3 times, knit to end. (104 sts)

Knit 4 rows.

Bind off.

Weave in ends. ■

STITCH KEY
- K on RS, p on WS
- P on RS, k on WS
- C4F: Sl 2 sts to cn and hold in front, k2, k2 from cn
- C4B: Sl 2 sts to cn and hold in back, k2, k2 from cn

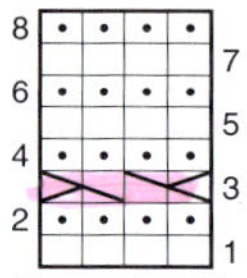

Rep Rows 1–8 for pat
LEFT CABLE

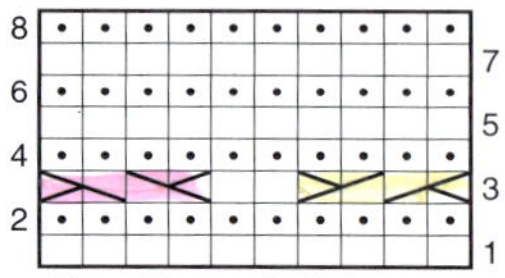

Rep Rows 1–8 for pat
CENTER CABLE

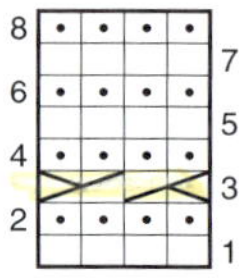

Rep Rows 1–8 for pat
RIGHT CABLE

Hugs & Kisses for Baby

SIZE
Approx 32 inches x 40 inches

MATERIALS
- Caron Simply Soft 100 percent acrylic worsted weight yarn (330 yds/170g per skein): 5 skeins soft blue #2615
- Size 10 (6mm) 32-inch circular knitting needle or size needed to obtain gauge
- Cable needle
- 12 stitch markers (optional to mark cable patterns)

4 MEDIUM

GAUGE
14 sts and 26 rows =4 inches/10 cm in garter st
To save time, take time to check gauge.

SPECIAL ABBREVIATION
C6F (Cable 6 Front): Sl next 3 sts to cn and hold in front of work, k3, k3 from cn.

PATTERN STITCH
X-Cable (worked over 6 sts)

Rows 1, 3, 5, 9, 11 and 13 (RS): Knit.

Rows 2, 4, 6, 8, 10 and 12: P2, k2, p2.

Row 7: C6F.

Row 14: P2, k2, p2.

PATTERN NOTES
Chart is provided for pat st for those preferring to work from a chart.

Circular needle used to accommodate large number of sts. Do not join; work back and forth in rows.

Stitch markers may be used, if desired, to mark rep of 6-st cable pat.

INSTRUCTIONS
Using long-tail cast-on, cast on 120 sts.

Lower Border
Knit 7 rows (4 ridges).

Body
Set up pat

Row 1: [K12, work Row 1 of X-Cable over next 6 sts] 6 times, k12.

Rows 2–14: Continue in established pat until 14 rows of cable pat are complete.

Row 15 (RS): K3, work Row 1 of X-Cable over next 6 sts, [k12, work Row 1 of X-Cable over next 6 sts] 6 times, k3.

Rows 16–28: Continue in established pat until 14 rows of cable are complete.

Row 29: [K12, work Row 1 of X-Cable over next 6 sts] 6 times, k12.

Rows 30–42: Continue in established pat until 14 rows of cable are complete.

Rows 43–56: Knit 14 rows.

Row 57 (RS): K3, work Row 1 of X-Cable over next 6 sts, knit to last 9 sts, work Row 1 of X-Cable over next 6 sts, k3.

Rows 58–70: Continue in established pat until 14 rows of cable are complete.

Rows 71–84: Knit 14 rows.

[Rep Rows 57–84] 5 times.

Rep Rows 1–42.

Upper Border
Knit 6 rows.

Bind off knitwise on RS row. ■

STITCH KEY
☐ K on RS, p on WS
⦿ P on RS, k on WS
C6F: Sl 3 sts to cn and hold in front, k3, k3 from cn

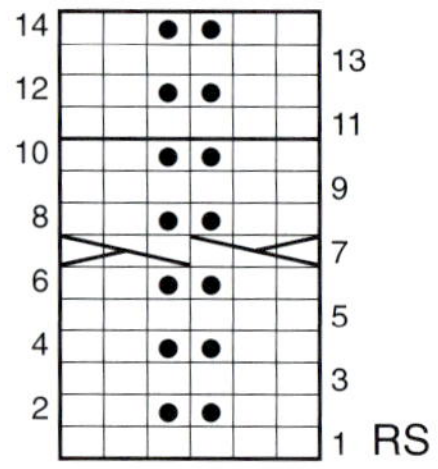

Rep Rows 1–14 for pat

X-CABLE

Stockinette Stitch Cabled Throw

SIZE
Approx 40 x 44 inches

MATERIALS
- Plymouth Encore Chunky 75 percent acrylic/25 percent wool bulky weight yarn (143 yds/100g per skein): 10 skeins grayish green #678
- Size 10½ (6.5mm) 32-inch circular and double-pointed needles
- Cable needle

5 BULKY

GAUGE
15 sts and 20 rows = 4 inches/10 cm in pat st
To save time, take time to check gauge.

SPECIAL ABBREVIATIONS
C6B (Cable 6 Back): Sl next 3 sts to cn and hold in back of work, k3, k3 from cn.

C6F (Cable 6 Front): Sl next 3 sts to cn and hold in front of work, k3, k3 from cn.

SPECIAL TECHNIQUE
Cable Cast On: *Insert RH needle between the last 2 sts on the LH needle. Knit a st and place it on the LH needle; rep from * for desired number of sts.

PATTERN STITCH
Stockinette Stitch Cables (multiple of 9 sts)

Row 1 and all WS rows: Purl.

Row 2: C6B, k3.

Rows 4, 6 and 10: Knit.

Row 8: K3, C6F.

Row 12: Purl.

Rep Rows 1–12 for pattern.

PATTERN NOTES
Chart is provided for pat st for those preferring to work from a chart. Row 1 is a WS row and is worked from left to right.

Circular needle used to accommodate large number of sts. Do not join; work back and forth in rows.

INSTRUCTIONS
Using long-tail cast-on, cast on 155 sts.

Row 1 (WS): K1, work Row 1 of Stockinette Stitch Cables pat across next 153 sts, k1.

Row 2: K1, work Row 2 of Stockinette Stitch Cables pat to last st, k1.

Continue in pat as established, keeping first and last sts in garter st, and rem sts in Stockinette Stitch Cables pat until piece measures approx 45 inches from beg, ending with Row 3 or Row 9 of pat. Do not bind off.

I-cord bind-off: Using cable cast-on, cast on 3 sts at beg of row. *K2, ssk, do not turn, sl 3 sts from RH needle to LH needle, bring yarn across back of work; rep from * until 3 sts rem. Change to double-pointed needles

Turn corner: [K3, slide sts to other end of needle, do not turn] twice.

Applied I-cord: Picking up sts evenly along next edge (approx 2 sts for every 3 rows), k3, pick up and knit 1 st from edge, slide sts to other end of needle, do not turn, bring yarn across back of work; *k2, ssk, pick up and knit 1 st from edge, slide sts to other end of needle; rep from * to corner. Continue to turn corners as before and work applied I-cord around rem 2 edges of piece. Do not bind off. Graft (see below) last 3 sts to first 3 sts. ■

STITCH KEY

- K on RS, p on WS
- C6F: Sl 3 sts to cn and hold in front, k3, k3 from cn
- C6B: Sl 3 sts to cn and hold in

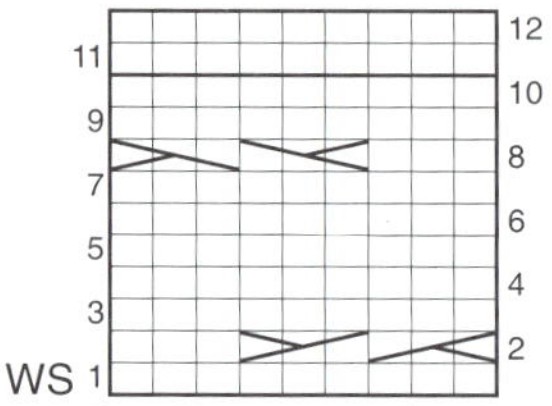

Rep Rows 1–12 for pat

STOCKINETTE STITCH CABLES

Kitchener Stitch

This method of weaving with two needles is used for the toes of socks and flat seams. To weave the edges together and form an unbroken line of stockinette stitch, divide all stitches evenly onto two knitting needles—one behind the other. Thread yarn into tapestry needle. Hold needles with wrong sides together and work from right to left as follows:

Step 1:
Insert tapestry needle into first stitch on front needle as to purl. Draw yarn through stitch, leaving stitch on knitting needle.

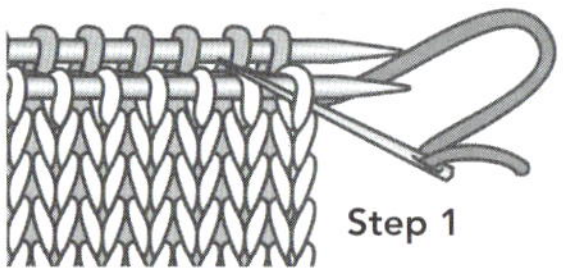

Step 2:
Insert tapestry needle into the first stitch on the back needle as to purl. Draw yarn through stitch and slip stitch off knitting needle.

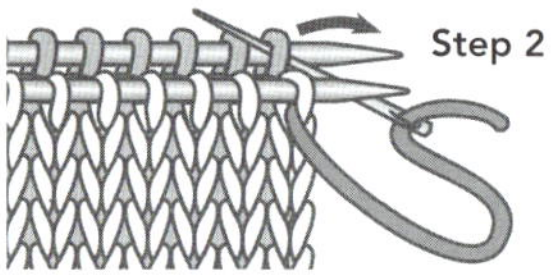

Step 3:
Insert tapestry needle into the next stitch on same (back) needle as to knit, leaving stitch on knitting needle.

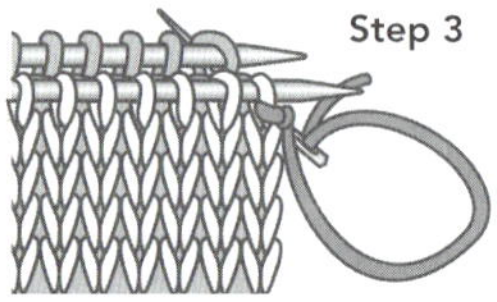

Step 4:
Insert tapestry needle into the first stitch on the front needle as to knit. Draw yarn through stitch and slip stitch off knitting needle.

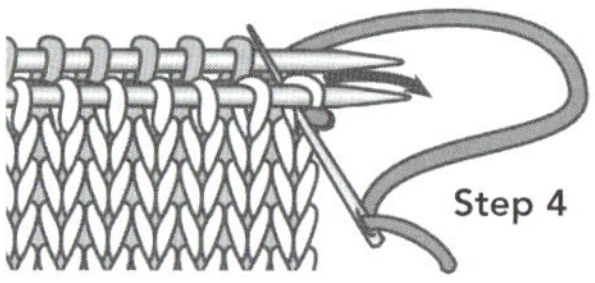

Step 5:
Insert tapestry needle into the next stitch on same (front) needle as to purl. Draw yarn through stitch, leaving stitch on knitting needle.

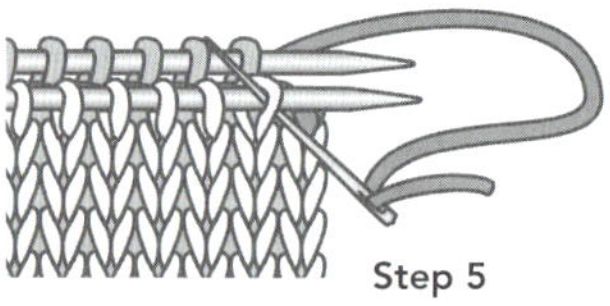

Repeat Steps 2 through 5 until one stitch is left on each needle. Then repeat Steps 2 and 4. Fasten off. Woven stitches should be the same size as adjacent knitted stitches.

Super-Sized Cables

SIZE
Approx 42 inches x 60 inches

MATERIALS
- Plymouth Encore Worsted 75 percent acrylic/25 percent wool worsted weight yarn (200 yds/100g per skein): 8 skeins tan #1203
- Size 9 (5.5mm) 32-inch circular knitting needle or size needed to obtain gauge
- Cable needle
- Stitch markers

GAUGE
16 sts and 21 rows = 4 inches/10 cm in St st
To save time, take time to check gauge.

SPECIAL ABBREVIATIONS
Pm (place marker): Place marker on needle.

M1 (Make 1): Insert LH needle from front to back into strand between st just worked and next st, k1-tbl.

C16F (Cable 16 Front): Sl next 8 sts onto cn and hold in front of work, k8, k8 from cn.

PATTERN STITCHES
A. Seed Stitch (even number of sts)

Row 1 (WS): *K1, p1; rep from * across.

Row 2: *P1, k1; rep from * across.

Rep Rows 1 and 2 for pat.

B. Super-Sized Cable (multiple of 16 sts)

Rows 1, 3, 5, 7, 9, 13, 15, 17, 19, 21 (RS): Knit.

Row 2 and all WS rows: Purl.

Row 11: C16F.

Row 22: Purl.

Rep Rows 1–22 for Super-Sized Cable pat.

PATTERN NOTES
Chart is provided for pat st for those preferring to work from chart.

Circular needle used to accommodate large number of sts. Do not join; work back and forth in rows.

INSTRUCTIONS

Cast on 164 sts.

Lower Border

Work 8 rows in Seed Stitch.

Inc row (WS): Work 8 sts in established Seed St, pm, k18, pm, [p1, M1] 8 times, pm, *k18, pm, work 8 sts in established Seed St, pm, k18, [p1, M1] 8 times, pm; rep from * once more, k18, pm work last 8 sts in established Seed St pat. (188 sts)

Body

Set-up Row (RS): *Work Seed St over next 8 sts, p18, work Row 1 of Super-Sized Cable over next 16 sts, p18; rep from * twice more, work Seed St to end.

STITCH KEY

☐ K on RS, p on WS

C16F: Sl 8 sts to cn and hold

Continue in pats as established, work even until piece measures approximately 58 inches long, ending with Row 21 of Super-Sized Cable.

Upper Border

Dec Row (WS): Removing markers, work 8 sts in Seed St, k18, [p2tog] 8 times, *k18, work 8 sts in established Seed St, k18, [p2tog] 8 times; rep from * once more, k18, work last 8 sts in established Seed St. (164 sts)

Work 7 rows even in Seed St.

Bind off in pat. ■

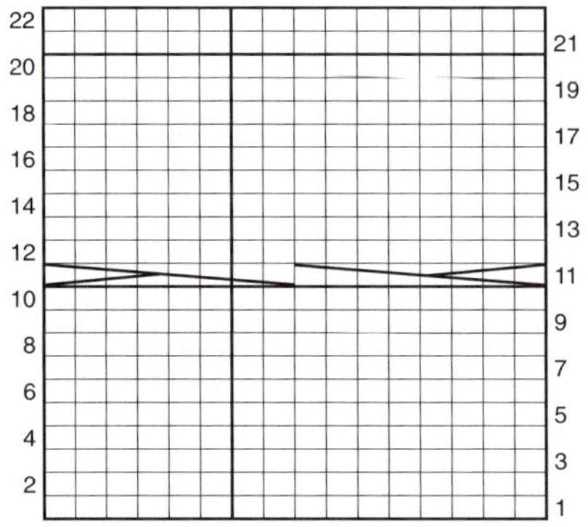

Rep Rows 1–22 for pat

SUPER-SIZED CABLE

Cables & Lace Throw

SIZE
Approx 36 inches x 44 inches

MATERIALS
- Berroco Comfort 50 percent super fine nylon/50 percent super fine acrylic worsted weight yarn (210 yds/100g per ball): 7 balls ivory #9701
- Size 10 (6mm) 32-inch circular knitting needle or size needed to obtain gauge
- Cable needle

4 MEDIUM

GAUGE
16 sts and 24 rows = 4 inches/10cm in St st
To save time, take time to check gauge.

PATTERN NOTES
Throw is worked following Cable & Lace chart. Instructions include 1 edge st at each side which is not shown on chart.

Circular needle is used to accommodate large number of sts. Do not join; work back and forth in rows.

INSTRUCTIONS
Cast on 176 sts.

K1, work Row 1 of Cable & Lace chart across next 174 sts, k1.

Keeping first and last sts in garter st and working center 174 sts following chart, work even until piece measures approx 44 inches, ending with either a Row 4 or Row 10 of chart.

Bind off in pattern.

Weave in ends. ■

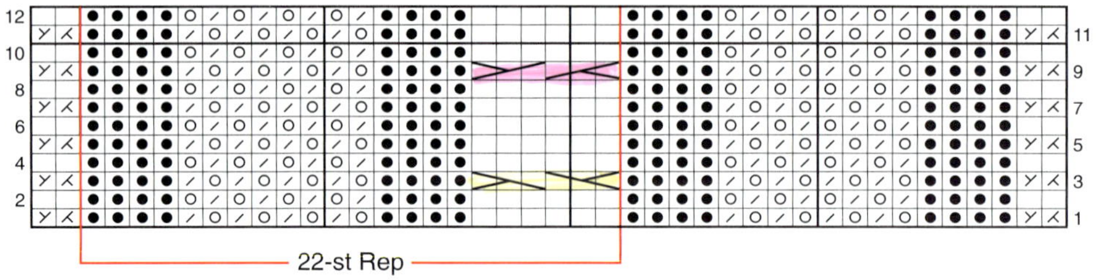

CABLE & LACE CHART

STITCH KEY

- K on RS, p on WS
- P on RS, k on WS
- Yo
- K2tog
- K2tog, leaving stitches on needle, knit first st again, sl both sts off LH needle
- Sl 3 sts to cn and hold in back, k3, k3 from cn
- Sl 3 sts to cn and hold in front, k3, k3 from cn

Comfy Ribbed Cables Throw

SIZE

Approx 44 inches x 60 inches

MATERIALS

- Berroco Comfort 50 percent super fine nylon/50 percent super fine acrylic worsted weight yarn (210 yds/100g per ball): 13 balls filbert #9745
- Size 9 (5.5 mm) 32-inch circular knitting needle or size needed to obtain gauge
- Cable needle

GAUGE

17 sts and 28 rows = 4 inches/10cm in Moss St
To save time, take time to check gauge.

PATTERN STITCHES

A. Moss Stitch (multiple of 4 sts +2)

Row 1 (RS): K2, *p2, k2; rep from * across.

Rows 2 and 3: P2, *k2, p2; rep from * across.

Row 4: K2, *p2, k2; rep from * across.

Rep Rows 1–4 for pat.

B. Ribbed Cable Panel (worked over 22 sts)

St pat is worked following chart.

Rep Rows 1–28 for pat.

PATTERN NOTE

First and last 2 sts are worked in garter st throughout.

INSTRUCTIONS

Cast on 226 sts.

Set up pat

K2, work Ribbed Cable Panel across next 22 sts, [work Moss St across next 28 sts, work Ribbed Cable Panel across next 22 sts] 4 times, k2.

Continue in pat as established until piece measures approximately 60 inches long, ending with Row 4 of Ribbed Cable Panel.

Bind off in pattern.

Weave in ends. ■

STITCH KEY

- K on RS, p on WS
- P on RS, k on WS
- Sl 3 sts to cn and hold in back, k3, k3 from cn
- Sl 2 sts to cn and hold in front, p1, k2 from cn
- Sl 1 st to cn and hold in back, k2, p1 from cn
- Sl 2 sts to cn and hold in back, k2, k2 from cn

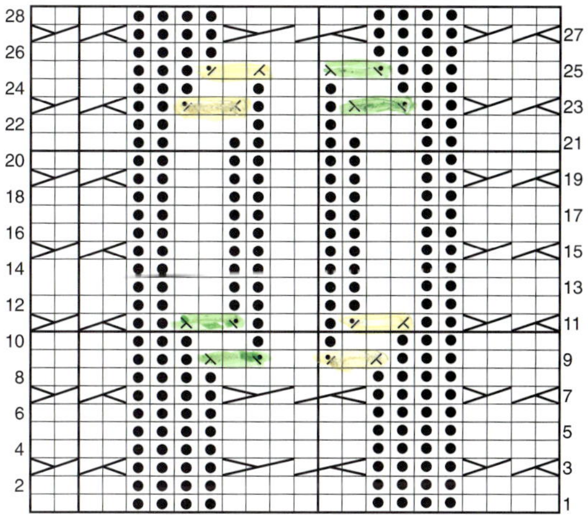

Rep Rows 1–28 for pat

RIBBED CABLE PANEL

Rose Aran Throw

SIZE

Approx 39 inches x 54 inches

MATERIALS

- Plymouth Encore Worsted 75 percent acrylic/25 percent wool worsted weight yarn (200 yds/100g per skein): 8 skeins raspberry #180
- Size 9 (5.5mm) 32-inch circular knitting needle, or size needed to obtain gauge
- Cable needle
- Stitch markers

GAUGE

15 sts and 22 rows = 4 inches/10cm in St st
To save time, take time to check gauge.

SPECIAL ABBREVIATIONS

M1 (Make 1): Insert LH needle from front to back into strand between st just worked and next st, k1-tbl.

C4B (Cable 4 Back): Sl next 2 sts onto cn and hold in back of work, k2, k2 from cn.

C4F (Cable 4 Front): Sl next 2 sts onto cn and hold in front of work, k2, k2 from cn.

C8B (Cable 8 Back): Sl next 4 sts onto cn and hold in back of work, k4, k4 from cn.

C8F (Cable 8 Front): Sl next 4 sts onto cn and hold in front of work, k4, k4 from cn.

PATTERN STITCHES

A. Moss St (multiple of 4 sts + 2)

Row 1 (RS): K2, *p2, k2; rep from * across.

Rows 2 and 3: P2, *k2, p2; rep from * across.

Row 4: K2, *p2, k2; rep from * across.

Rep Rows 1–4 for pat.

B. Right Twist (multiple of 2 sts)

Row 1 (RS): K2tog, keeping sts on needle; knit second st again and slip both sts off needle.

Row 2: Purl.

Rep Rows 1 and 2 for pat.

C. Honeycomb Cable (multiple of 12 sts)

Rows 1 (RS): P2, C4B, C4F, p2.

Row 2 and all WS rows: K2, p8, k2.

Row 3: P2, k8, p2.

Row 5: P2, C4F, C4B, p2.

Row 7: Rep Row 3.

Row 8: K2, p8, k2.

Rep Rows 1–8 for pat.

D. Right-Cross Cable (multiple of 12 sts)

Rows 1, 5 and 7 (RS): P2, k8, p2.

Row 1, 5, 7: P2, k8, P2

Row 2 and all WS rows: K2, p8, k2.

Row 3: P2, C8B, p2.

Row 8: K2, p8, k2.

Rep Rows 1–8 for pat.

E. Left-Cross Cable (multiple of 12 sts)

Rows 1, 5 and 7 (RS): P2, k8, p2.

Row 2 and all WS rows: K2, p8, k2.

Row 3: P2, C8F, p2.

Row 8: K2, p8, k2.

Rep Rows 1–8 for pat.

F. Diamond Panel (multiple of 49 sts)

Work 49 sts of Diamond Panel as shown on Chart.

PATTERN NOTES

Charts are provided for pat sts for those preferring to work from a chart.

Circular needle used to accommodate large number of sts. Do not join; work back and forth in rows.

Sl the first st of every row purlwise. Knit the last st of every row.

INSTRUCTIONS

Lower Border

Cast on 164 sts.

Row 1 (RS): Sl 1 purlwise, work Moss St pat across next 162 sts, k1.

Continuing to sl the first st and knit the last st of each row, work 6 more rows in Moss St pat.

Inc row (WS): Sl 1 purlwise, work 10 sts in Moss St pat as established, p2, k2, [p1, M1] 4 times, *k2,

honeycomb

cross cable

p2, work next 6 sts in Moss St pat as established, p2, k2, [p1, M1] 4 times; rep from * once more; k2, p2, k21, [p1, M1] 3 times, p1, k21; **p2, k2, [p1, M1] 4 times, k2, p2, work next 6 sts in Moss St pat as established; rep from ** once more; p2, k2, [p1, M1] 4 times, k2, p2, work next 10 sts in Moss St pat as established, k1. (191 sts)

Body

Continue to sl the first st and knit the last st of each row.

Set-up Row (RS): Sl 1 purlwise, working Row 1 of each pat across, work 10 sts in Moss St pat as established; *Right Twist over next 2 sts, Honeycomb Cable over next 12 sts, Right Twist over next 2 sts, work 6 sts Moss St pat as established; rep from * once more; Right Twist over next 2 sts, Right-Cross Cable over next 12 sts, Right Twist over next 2 sts, Diamond Panel over next 49 sts, Right Twist over next 2 sts, Left-Cross Cable over next 12 sts, Right Twist over next 2 sts; ** work 6 sts in Moss St pat as established, Right Twist over next 2 sts, Honeycomb Cable over next 12 sts, Right Twist over next 2 sts; rep from ** once more, work 10 sts in Moss St pat as established, k1.

Continue in established patterns until Row 50 of Diamond Panel is complete, then continue in established patterns working [Rows 3–50 of Diamond Panel] 4 times, then continue in established patterns working Rows 3–54 of Diamond Panel, ending with Row 6 of Right- and Left-Cross Cables and Row 6 of Honeycomb Cable.

Upper Border

Dec Row (WS): Work 10 sts in Moss St pat as established, p2, k2, [k2tog] 4 times; *k2, p2, work 6 sts in established Moss St pat, p2, k2, [k2tog] 4 times; rep from * once more; k2, p2, k21, [k2tog] 3 times, p1, k21, **p2, k2, [k2tog] 4 times, k2, p2, work 6 sts in established Moss St pat; rep from ** once more; p2, k2, [k2tog] 4 times, p2, k2, work 10 sts in established Moss St pat. (164 sts)

Continuing to sl the first st and knit the last st of each row, work 8 rows even in established Moss St pat.

Bind off. ■

STITCH KEY

HONEYCOMB, LEFT- AND RIGHT-CROSS CABLES

- K on RS, P on WS
- P on RS, k on WS
- C4B: Sl 2 sts to cn and hold in back, k2, k2 from cn
- C4F: Sl 2 sts to cn and hold in front, k2, k2 from cn
- C8B: Sl 4 sts to cn and hold in back, k4, k4 from cn
- C8F: Sl 4 sts to cn and hold in front, k4, k4 from cn

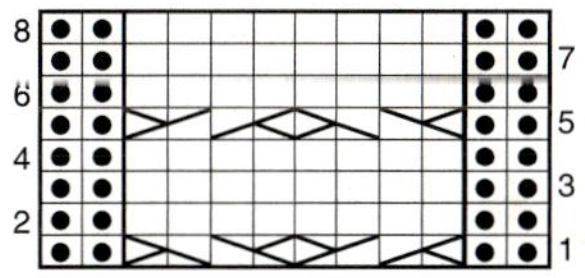
Rep Rows 1–8 for pat

HONEYCOMB CABLE

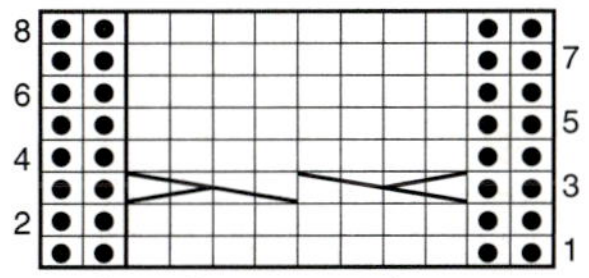
Rep Rows 1–8 for pat

LEFT-CROSS CABLE

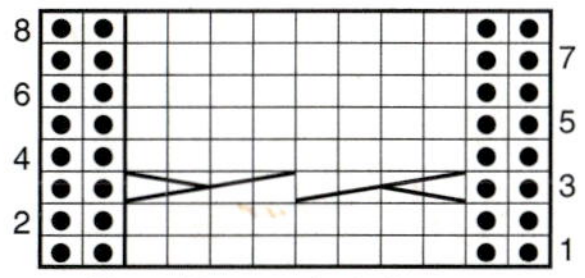
Rep Rows 1–8 for pat

RIGHT-CROSS CABLE

Border
R twist
Honey Comb
R twist
moss
R Twist
Honey comb
R twist
moss

R Twist
diamond panel
R twist
L cross
R twist
moss
R Twist

STITCH KEY

DIAMOND PANEL

- K on RS, p on WS
- P on RS, k on WS
- Sl 3 sts to cn and hold in front, p1, k3 from cn
- Sl 1 st to cn and hold in back, k3, p1 from cn
- Sl 3 sts to cn and hold in front, k1, k3 from cn
- Sl 1 st to cn and hold in back, k3, k1 from cn
- Sl 3 sts to cn and hold in back, k4, k3 from cn

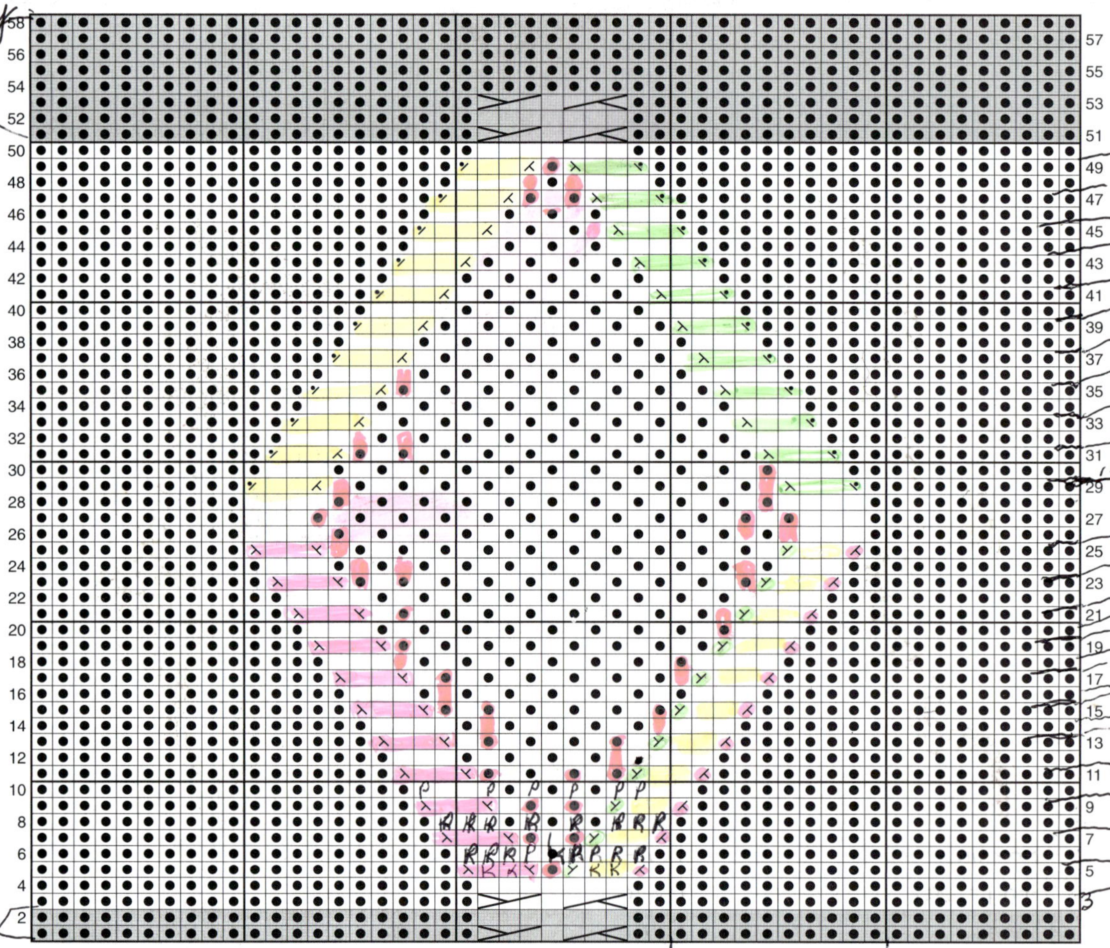

Work Rows 3–50 six times

DIAMOND PANEL

Inches into Millimeters & Centimeters

All measurements are rounded off slightly.

inches	mm	cm	inches	cm	inches	cm	inches	cm	inches	cm
⅛	3	0.3	3	7.5	13	33.0	26	66.0	39	99.0
¼	6	0.6	3½	9.0	14	35.5	27	68.5	40	101.5
⅜	10	1.0	4	10.0	15	38.0	28	71.0	41	104.0
½	13	1.3	4½	11.5	16	40.5	29	73.5	42	106.5
⅝	15	1.5	5	12.5	17	43.0	30	76.0	43	109.0
¾	20	2.0	5½	14	18	46.0	31	79.0	44	112.0
⅞	22	2.2	6	15.0	19	48.5	32	81.5	45	114.5
1	25	2.5	7	18.0	20	51.0	33	84.0	46	117.0
1¼	32	3.8	8	20.5	21	53.5	34	86.5	47	119.5
1½	38	3.8	9	23.0	22	56.0	35	89.0	48	122.0
1¾	45	4.5	10	25.5	23	58.5	36	91.5	49	124.5
2	50	5.0	11	28.0	24	61.0	37	94.0	50	127.0
2½	65	6.5	12	30.5	25	63.5	38	96.5		

Knitting Needles Conversion Chart

U.S.	1	2	3	4	5	6	7	8	9	10	10½	11	13	15	17	19	35	50
Continental-mm	2.25	2.75	3.25	3.5	3.75	4	4.5	5	5.5	6	6.5	8	9	10	12.75	15	19	25

Glossary

bind off—used to finish an edge

cast on—process of making foundation stitches used in knitting

decrease—means of reducing the number of stitches in a row

increase—means of adding to the number of stitches in a row

intarsia—method of knitting a multicolored pattern into the fabric

knitwise—insert needle into stitch as if to knit

long tail cast on—method of cast-on where length of yarn about an inch long for each stitch is left at end before making first cast-on stitch

make 1—method of increasing using the strand between the last stitch worked and the next stitch

place marker—placing a purchased marker or loop of contrasting yarn onto the needle for ease in working a pattern repeat

purlwise—insert needle into stitch as if to purl

right side—side of garment or piece that will be seen when worn

selvage stitch—edge stitch used to make seaming easier

slip, slip, knit—method of decreasing by moving stitches from left needle to right needle and working them together

slip stitch—an unworked stitch slipped from left needle to right needle, usually as if to purl

work even—continue to work in the pattern as established without working any increases or decreases

work in pattern as established—continue to work following the pattern stitch as it has been set up or established on the needle, working any increases or decreases in such a way that the established pattern remains the same

yarn over—method of increasing by wrapping the yarn over the right needle without working a stitch

Standard Yarn Weight System

Categories of yarn, gauge ranges, and recommended needle sizes

Yarn Weight Symbol & Category Names	1 SUPER FINE	2 FINE	3 LIGHT	4 MEDIUM	5 BULKY	6 SUPER BULKY
Type of Yarns in Category	Sock, Fingering, Baby	Sport, Baby	DK, Light Worsted	Worsted, Afghan, Aran	Chunky, Craft, Rug	Bulky, Roving
Knit Gauge* Ranges in Stockinette Stitch to 4 inches	21–32 sts	23–26 sts	21–24 sts	16–20 sts	12–15 sts	6–11 sts
Recommended Needle in Metric Size Range	2.25–3.25mm	3.25–3.75mm	3.75–4.5mm	4.5–5.5mm	5.5–8mm	8mm
Recommended Needle U.S. Size Range	1 to 3	3 to 5	5 to 7	7 to 9	9 to 11	11 and larger

* GUIDELINES ONLY: The above reflect the most commonly used gauges and needle sizes for specific yarn categories.

Meet the Designer

Designer Edie Eckman has her hands in many aspects of the fiber arts—teaching, writing, designing and editing. Her designs are contemporary classics accessible to the average knitter or crocheter, and they have appeared in many books, magazines, pattern leaflets and yarn company publications. Edie travels extensively to teach at conventions, shops and guilds.

She is the author of numerous ASN publications such as *Learn to Knit Cables*, *Knit a Dozen Beanies* and *Learn to Knit Socks*. She is also the author of *The Crochet Answer Book* and *Beyond the Square Crochet Motifs* (Storey Publishing).

Edie grew up in Georgia and learned to knit literally at the knee of her live-in grandmother. She now lives in the Shenandoah Valley of Virginia with her husband, two children, a dog and a vast yarn stash.

E-mail: Customer_Service@whitebirches.com

HOUSE of WHITE BIRCHES
PUBLISHERS SINCE 1947

Easy Cable Throws is published by DRG, 306 East Parr Road, Berne, IN 46711, telephone (260) 589-4000. Printed in USA.

RETAIL STORES: If you would like to carry this pattern book or any other DRG publications, call the Wholesale Department at Annie's Attic to set up a direct account: (903) 636-4303. Also, request a complete listing of publications available from DRG.

ISBN: 978-1-59217-230-6
1 2 3 4 5 6 7 8 9

STAFF
Editor: Jeanne Stauffer
Managing Editor: Dianne Schmidt
Technical Artist: Kathy Wesley
Copy Supervisor: Michelle Beck
Copy Editor: Susanna Tobias
Graphic Arts Supervisor: Ronda Bechinski
Graphic Artists: Pam Gregory, Erin Augsburger
Art Director: Brad Snow
Assistant Art Director: Nick Pierce
Photography Supervisor: Tammy Christian
Photography: Matt Owen
Photo Stylist: Tammy Steiner